I0804268

AMAZING MIGRATIONS

ON THE MOVE WITH ADÉLIE PENGUINS

by Rebecca Donnelly
illustrated by Alan Brown

GRASSHOPPER

Tools for Parents & Teachers

Grasshopper Books enhance imagination and introduce the earliest readers to fiction with fun storylines and illustrations. The easy-to-read text supports early reading experiences with repetitive sentence patterns and sight words.

Before Reading

- Discuss the cover illustration. What do readers see?
- Look at the glossary together. Discuss the words.

Read the Book

- Read the book to the child, or have him or her read independently.
- "Walk" through the book and look at the illustrations. Who is the main character? What is happening in the story?

After Reading

- Prompt the child to think more. Ask: Why do Adélie penguins migrate? Can you name any other animals that migrate?

Grasshopper Books are published by Jump!
5357 Penn Avenue South
Minneapolis, MN 55419
www.jumplibrary.com

Copyright © 2023 Jump! International copyright reserved in all countries. No part of this book may be reproduced in any form without written permission from the publisher.

Library of Congress Cataloging-in-Publication Data

Names: Donnelly, Rebecca, author.
Brown, Alan, illustrator.
Title: On the move with Adélie penguins
Rebecca Donnelly; illustrated by Alan Brown.
Description: Minneapolis, MN: Jump!, Inc., [2023]
Series: Amazing migrations | Includes index.
Audience: Ages 7-10
Identifiers: LCCN 2021060750 (print)
LCCN 2021060751 (ebook)
ISBN 9781636908762 (hardcover)
ISBN 9781636908779 (paperback)
ISBN 9781636908786 (ebook)
Subjects: LCSH: Adélie penguin–Migration–
Juvenile literature.
Migratory animals–Juvenile literature.
Classification: LCC QL696.S473 D66 2023 (print)
LCC QL696.S473 (ebook)
DDC 598.47–dc23/eng/20220110
LC record available at https://lccn.loc.gov/2021060750
LC ebook record available at https://lccn.loc.gov/2021060751

Editor: Eliza Leahy
Direction and Layout: Anna Peterson
Illustrator: Alan Brown

Printed in the United States of America at
Corporate Graphics in North Mankato, Minnesota.

Table of Contents

Antarctic Adventure

Hi, I'm Adam. I'm an Adélie penguin. I'm swimming back to my nesting site in Antarctica after a long winter migration through the Southern Ocean.

Last year, I built a nest on this rocky beach. Here it is! It needs a little work before it is ready for eggs again.

The other members of my colony are back, too. Anya is my mate. We migrate separately, but every spring, we meet at the same nesting site. I build the nest again. Anya checks my work!

Not all penguins make it back to their nesting sites in spring. Some of my friends have to find new mates this year. Life is tough out here!

Anya

After a few weeks, mama penguins start laying eggs. Look, Anya laid two eggs!

Summer in Antarctica is cold and windy. Brr! Anya and I take turns sitting on our eggs. We keep them warm and safe from predators.

After one month, our chicks hatch. It's time to feed them. They eat fish and krill, but they can't swim yet. It's my turn to bring them food. Anya stays with them. Watch out for skua, Anya!

skua
chick

I bring food back to our chicks. They gobble it out of my beak!

Winter is coming. It will be cold and dark. We need sunlight and open water to find food. So it's time for the colony to migrate north.

We all leave at the same time, but families don't migrate together. We travel to the edge of the ice. Some of us slide on our bellies. It's called tobogganing. *Whee!*

One slides into the ocean. The rest of us follow. If we swim in a group, it's harder for leopard seals to catch us.

We move north as more sea ice forms. We swim to find food, but we stay near the ice for safety.

Our winter migration lasts six months. We travel up to 8,000 miles (12,800 kilometers)! When spring comes, the ice starts to melt. We migrate south, back to our nesting site.

Last year's chicks won't come back to the nesting site until they are three to five years old. Then they have chicks of their own.

We made it! I need to fix my nest quickly before Anya comes back. If she likes it, we will have more chicks. And soon, they will learn to migrate, too!

Range Map

In winter, Adélie penguins swim north. They return to Antarctica in spring. Take a look at where they nest!

= Adélie penguin nesting sites

Let's Review!

Why do Adam and the other penguins in his colony leave their nesting site each winter?

A. to avoid predators
B. to find food
C. to avoid snow
D. to find new mates

Glossary

chicks: Young Adélie penguins.

colony: A group of penguins who live together.

krill: Small crustaceans that live in the ocean.

mate: One of the breeding partners of a pair of animals.

migration: The movement of animals from one area to another.

nesting site: A place chosen by a bird to build its nest and lay eggs.

predators: Animals that hunt other animals for food.

sea ice: Ice that forms as the ocean freezes in winter. Some sea ice lasts year-round.

skua: Seabirds that hunt Adélie penguins.

tobogganing: A fast way of traveling on snow and ice. To toboggan, penguins lie on their bellies and push themselves forward with their feet.

Let's Review! Answer Key: **B.** to find food

Index

To Learn More

FACT SURFER

Finding more information is as easy as 1, 2, 3.

1. Go to www.factsurfer.com
2. Enter "**onthemovewithAdéliepenguins**" into the search box.
3. Choose your book to see a list of websites.